U.S.A. TRAVEL GUIDES

VIRGINIA

BY ANN HEINRICHS • ILLUSTRATED BY MATT KANIA

The Child's World®
childsworld.com

Published by The Child's World®
1980 Lookout Drive • Mankato, MN 56003-1705
800-599-READ • www.childsworld.com

Photo Credits
Photographs ©: Daniel M. Silva/Shutterstock Images,
cover, 1; iStockphoto, 7, 8, 16, 20, 27; Petty Officer 3rd.
Class Mark Jones/U.S. Coast Guard, 11; C. Van Dyke/
Shutterstock Images, 12; National Park Service, 15, 24;
T. Johnson/Library of Congress, 17; Barry Blackburn/
Shutterstock Images, 19; Rex Bowman/Richmond Times-
Dispatch/AP Images, 23; Alex Brandon/AP Images, 28;
SuperStock/Glow Images, 31; Douglas Graham/CQ Roll
Call/AP Images, 32; Jay Yuan/Shutterstock Images, 35;
Shutterstock Images, 37 (top), 37 (bottom)

ISBN 9781503819863
LCCN 2016961198

Printing
Printed in the United States of America
PA02334

Ann Heinrichs is the author of more than 100 books for children and young adults. She has also enjoyed successful careers as a children's book editor and an advertising copywriter. Ann grew up in Fort Smith, Arkansas, and lives in Chicago, Illinois.

post card

About the Author
Ann Heinrichs

Matt Kania loves maps and, as a kid, dreamed of making them. In school he studied geography and cartography, and today he makes maps for a living. Matt's favorite thing about drawing maps is learning about the places they represent. Many of the maps he has created can be found in books, magazines, videos, Web sites, and public places.

post card

About the
Map Illustrator
Matt Kania

On the cover: Thomas Jefferson built his home, Monticello, in Charlottesville.

OUR VIRGINIA TRIP

VIRGINIA

Let's take a tour through Virginia! There's so much you can explore there.

You'll build sand castles. You'll watch wild ponies swimming. You'll visit a potato chip factory and meet Thomas Jefferson. You'll hang out with soldiers from the 1700s. You'll do farm chores and see great inventions. And you'll gaze at massive rock formations.

Just follow that loopy dotted line. Or just skip around. Either way, you're in for a great ride. Now hop aboard and buckle up. We're on our way through Virginia!

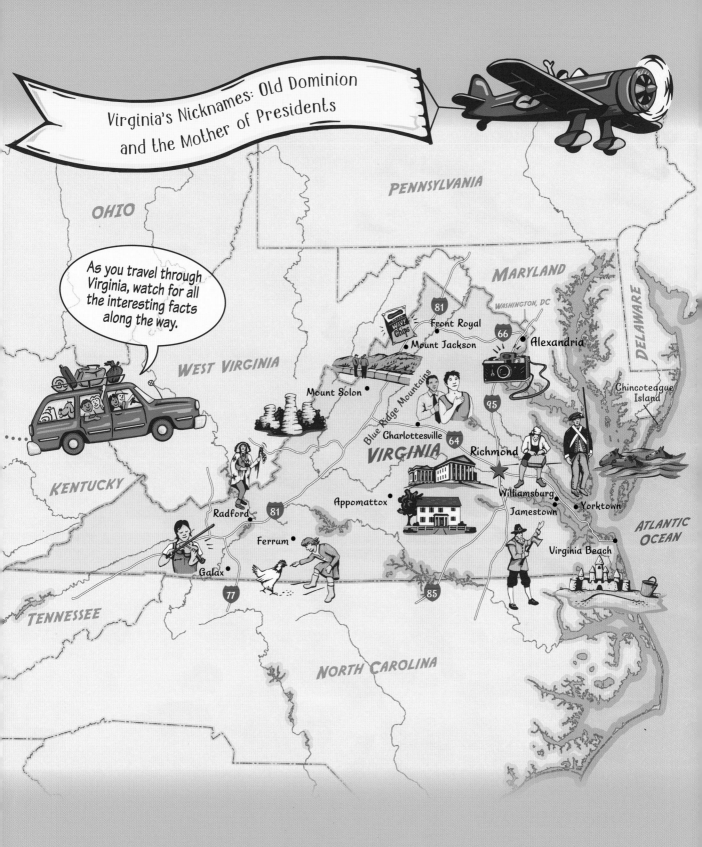

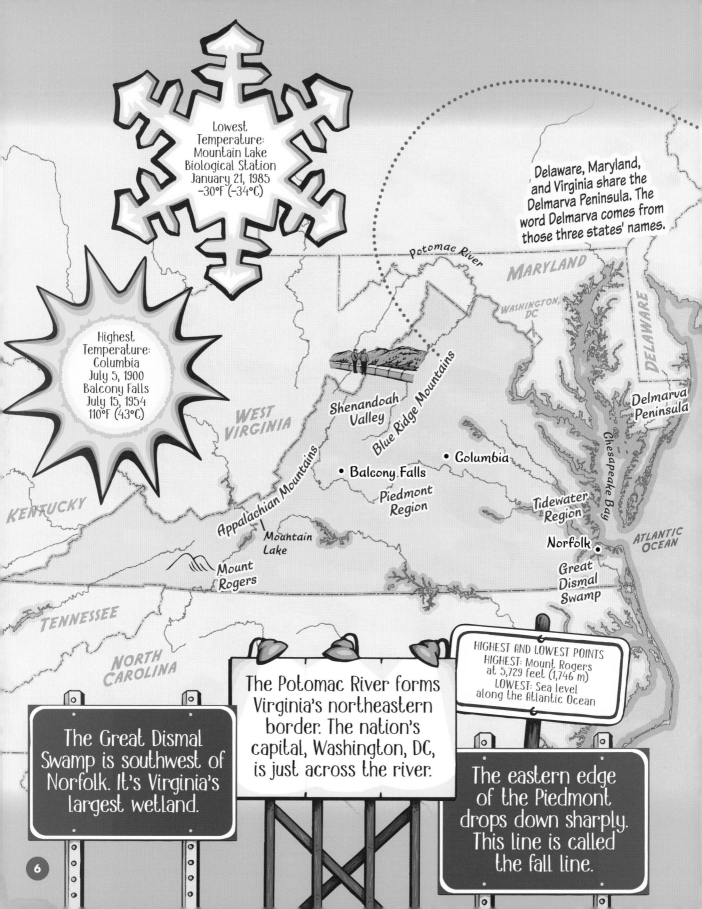

Lowest Temperature:
Mountain Lake Biological Station
January 21, 1985
–30°F (–34°C)

Delaware, Maryland, and Virginia share the Delmarva Peninsula. The word Delmarva comes from those three states' names.

Highest Temperature:
Columbia
July 5, 1900
Balcony Falls
July 15, 1954
110°F (43°C)

Potomac River

MARYLAND

WASHINGTON, DC

DELAWARE

Delmarva Peninsula

WEST VIRGINIA

Shenandoah Valley

Blue Ridge Mountains

Chesapeake Bay

KENTUCKY

Appalachian Mountains

Balcony Falls

Columbia

Piedmont Region

Tidewater Region

Norfolk

ATLANTIC OCEAN

Mountain Lake

Mount Rogers

Great Dismal Swamp

TENNESSEE

NORTH CAROLINA

HIGHEST AND LOWEST POINTS
HIGHEST: Mount Rogers at 5,729 feet (1,746 m)
LOWEST: Sea level along the Atlantic Ocean

The Great Dismal Swamp is southwest of Norfolk. It's Virginia's largest wetland.

The Potomac River forms Virginia's northeastern border. The nation's capital, Washington, DC, is just across the river.

The eastern edge of the Piedmont drops down sharply. This line is called the fall line.

SKYLINE DRIVE IN THE BLUE RIDGE MOUNTAINS

What a view! You're winding down Skyline Drive. It runs along the top of the Blue Ridge Mountains. You pass ragged cliffs and forested mountainsides. Far below is the beautiful Shenandoah Valley.

Western Virginia lies within the Appalachian Mountain range. The Blue Ridge Mountains are in this range. The Piedmont Region covers central Virginia. It has many hills and rolling plains.

Eastern Virginia is called the Tidewater Region. Virginia has a long, ragged coastline. It faces Chesapeake Bay and the Atlantic Ocean. Across Chesapeake Bay is the Delmarva **Peninsula**.

Enjoy breathtaking views from the Blue Ridge Mountains.

CHIMNEYS, TUNNELS, AND CAVES

Do they look like giant chimneys? Or castle towers? Visit Natural Chimneys Regional Park and see what you think. These rock towers are awesome!

Natural Chimneys is near Mount Solon. It's one of Virginia's many natural wonders. Another is Natural Tunnel, near Gate City. A creek cut this tunnel through the mountains. Natural Bridge, near the town of Natural Bridge, is a huge rock arch.

Underground streams created Virginia's many caverns, or caves. You'll find several caverns in the Shenandoah Valley. One is Grand Caverns, near Grottoes. Other caverns include Luray, Skyline, and Endless.

Some people make a wish and toss coins into Virginia's cave pools.

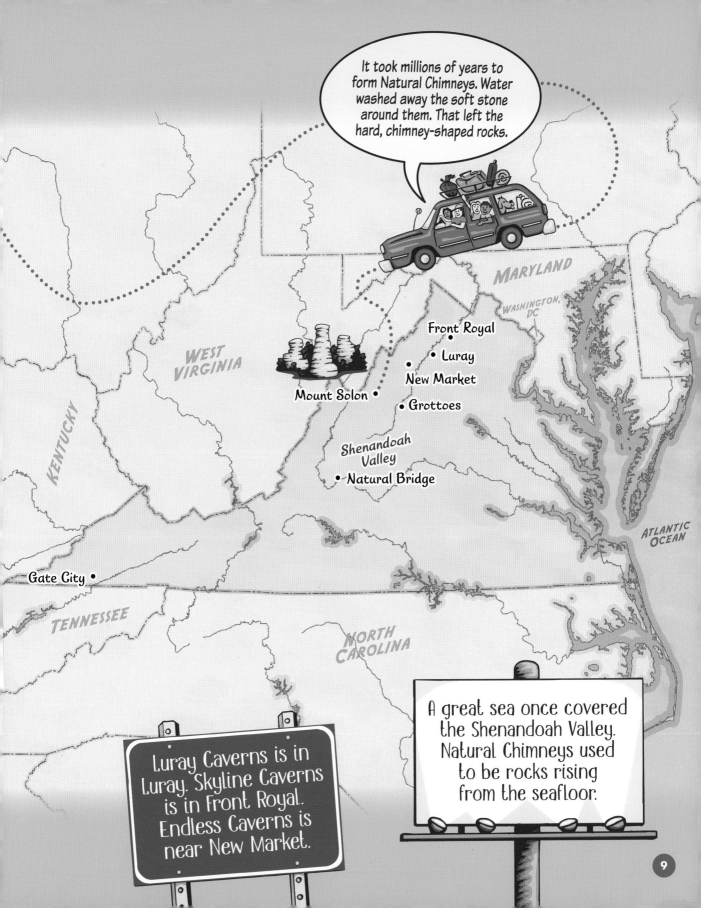

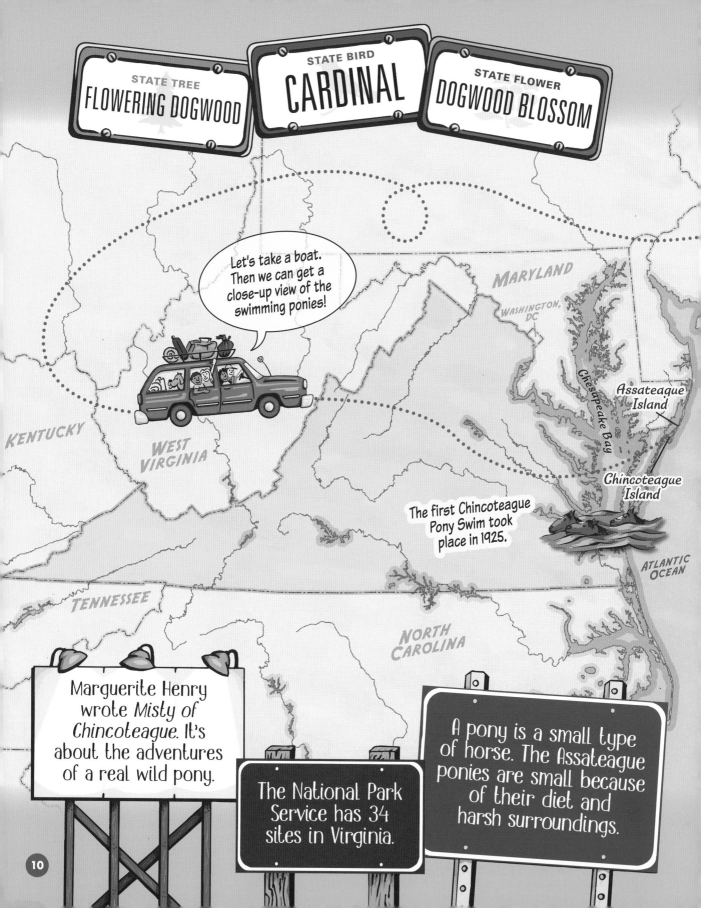

STATE TREE
FLOWERING DOGWOOD

STATE BIRD
CARDINAL

STATE FLOWER
DOGWOOD BLOSSOM

Let's take a boat. Then we can get a close-up view of the swimming ponies!

MARYLAND

WASHINGTON, DC

Chesapeake Bay

Assateague Island

KENTUCKY

WEST VIRGINIA

Chincoteague Island

The first Chincoteague Pony Swim took place in 1925.

ATLANTIC OCEAN

TENNESSEE

NORTH CAROLINA

Marguerite Henry wrote *Misty of Chincoteague*. It's about the adventures of a real wild pony.

The National Park Service has 34 sites in Virginia.

A pony is a small type of horse. The Assateague ponies are small because of their diet and harsh surroundings.

THE CHINCOTEAGUE WILD PONY SWIM

U. S. COAST GUARD

Splash! The wild ponies jump into the water. They churn up the water as they swim. At last, they climb ashore.

These frisky ponies live on Assateague Island. Once a year, the ponies are rounded up. Then they swim across to Chincoteague Island. There they are sold. This keeps a limit on the pony population.

Many animals live in Virginia's forests. They include deer, beavers, bobcats, foxes, and raccoons. Black bears live in the mountains.

The coastal wetlands are home to ducks and geese. Crabs, oysters, and clams live along Chesapeake Bay. Whales and dolphins swim in the Atlantic Ocean.

The U.S. Coast Guard keeps boaters away from the swimming ponies.

THE NATIVE AMERICAN HERITAGE FESTIVAL

Dancers in feathers and fringes stomp and swirl around. The drummers keep up a steady beat. Meanwhile, delicious smells drift from the food stands. You're attending the Native American Heritage Festival. It takes place in Radford.

Before Europeans arrived, Virginia was home to many Native Americans. Many spoke Algonquian, Siouan, and Iroquoian languages. Some lived along the coast. They caught fish and gathered shellfish. Others lived in the hilly Piedmont Region. The Occaneechi people lived in the Piedmont. They settled on an island in the Roanoke River.

Today, most Occaneechi live in North Carolina. There are 11 Native American nations still in Virginia. These include the Chickahominy, the Mattaponi, and the Rappahannock.

Some Rappahannocks teach people about traditional Rappahannock culture.

Who Lived Here before Europeans Arrived? Cherokee, Manahoac, Monacan, Nahyssan, Nottoway, Occaneechi, Powhatan, and Susquehannock

MARYLAND

WASHINGTON, DC

WEST VIRGINIA

KENTUCKY

The Chickahominy Fall Festival and Powwow takes place in Providence Forge.

Providence Forge

Piedmont Region

Roanoke River

ATLANTIC OCEAN

Let's get there for the grand entry procession! All of the dancers wear their traditional dress.

Radford

John H. Kerr Reservoir

NORTH CAROLINA

Occoneechee State Park is on Buggs Island Lake. That's Virginia's largest lake. It's also called John H. Kerr Reservoir.

The Occaneechi lived on an island in the Roanoke River from about 1250 to 1670.

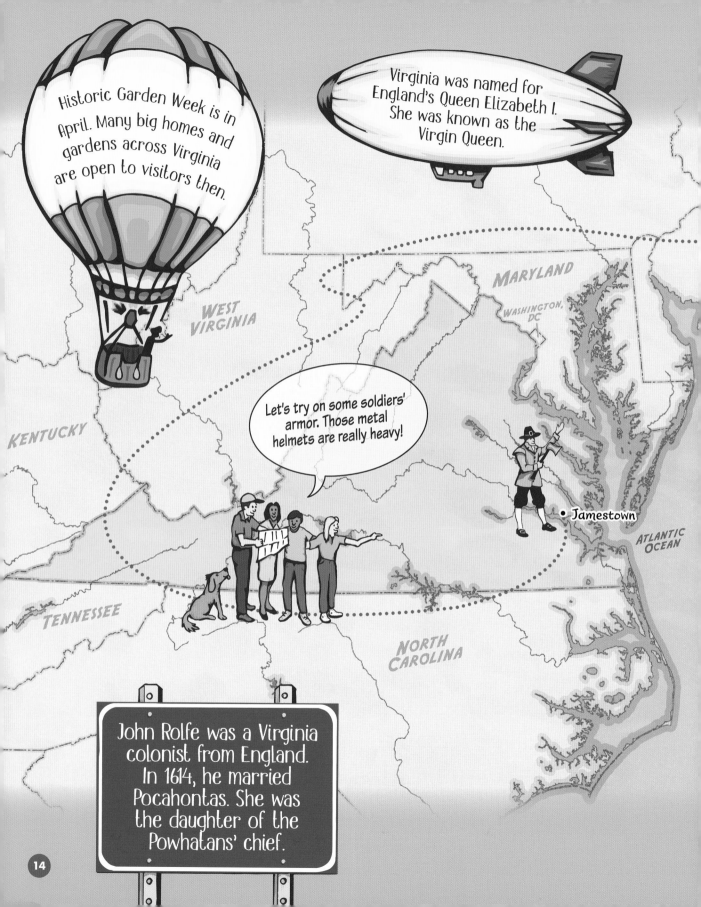

Historic Garden Week is in April. Many big homes and gardens across Virginia are open to visitors then.

Virginia was named for England's Queen Elizabeth I. She was known as the Virgin Queen.

Let's try on some soldiers' armor. Those metal helmets are really heavy!

John Rolfe was a Virginia colonist from England. In 1614, he married Pocahontas. She was the daughter of the Powhatans' chief.

MARYLAND

WASHINGTON, DC

WEST VIRGINIA

KENTUCKY

• Jamestown

ATLANTIC OCEAN

TENNESSEE

NORTH CAROLINA

JAMESTOWN SETTLEMENT

Climb aboard a sailing ship. Then watch blacksmiths and carpenters at work. You're exploring Jamestown Settlement!

English settlers arrived nearby in 1607. They set up the Virginia **Colony**. In time, there would be 13 English colonies. Jamestown was the colonies' first permanent settlement.

Eventually thousands of **colonists** settled near the coast. They began raising tobacco and other crops. Virginia formed its own colonial government. Most leaders were wealthy farmers. Many farmers owned plantations, or huge farms. By the 1670s, they enslaved African people and made them do the farm work. Many slave holders abused and mistreated the enslaved people.

This building frame in Jamestown shows how buildings were made.

COLONIAL WILLIAMSBURG

The shoemaker sews leather by hand. The **apothecary** offers cures for aches and pains. The print shop prints colonial newspapers. Other merchants make fancy hats and wigs. You're back in the 1700s at Colonial Williamsburg!

Williamsburg was a bustling city in colonial times. It became Virginia's capital in 1699. Colonial leaders made many important decisions there. They passed the Virginia Declaration of Rights in 1776. It promised basic freedoms to all citizens.

Virginia's General Court held sessions in Williamsburg, too. Plantation owners and other colonists came from miles around to attend. They did business with the many local merchants.

Step back in time at Colonial Williamsburg.

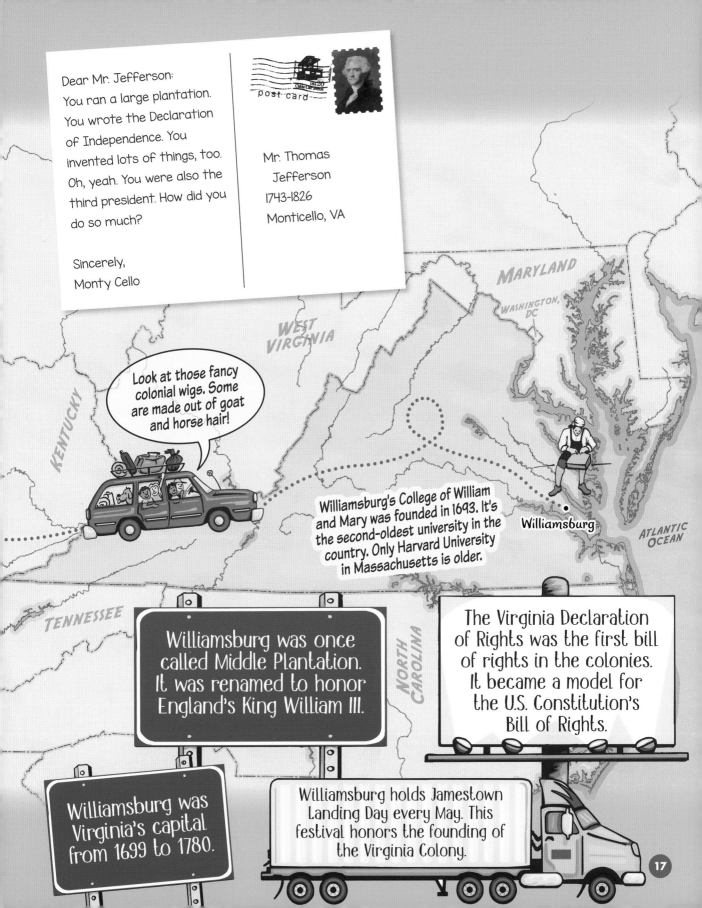

Dear Mr. Jefferson:
You ran a large plantation. You wrote the Declaration of Independence. You invented lots of things, too. Oh, yeah. You were also the third president. How did you do so much?

Sincerely,
Monty Cello

Mr. Thomas
  Jefferson
1743-1826
Monticello, VA

post card

Look at those fancy colonial wigs. Some are made out of goat and horse hair!

Williamsburg's College of William and Mary was founded in 1693. It's the second-oldest university in the country. Only Harvard University in Massachusetts is older.

Williamsburg

Williamsburg was once called Middle Plantation. It was renamed to honor England's King William III.

The Virginia Declaration of Rights was the first bill of rights in the colonies. It became a model for the U.S. Constitution's Bill of Rights.

Williamsburg was Virginia's capital from 1699 to 1780.

Williamsburg holds Jamestown Landing Day every May. This festival honors the founding of the Virginia Colony.

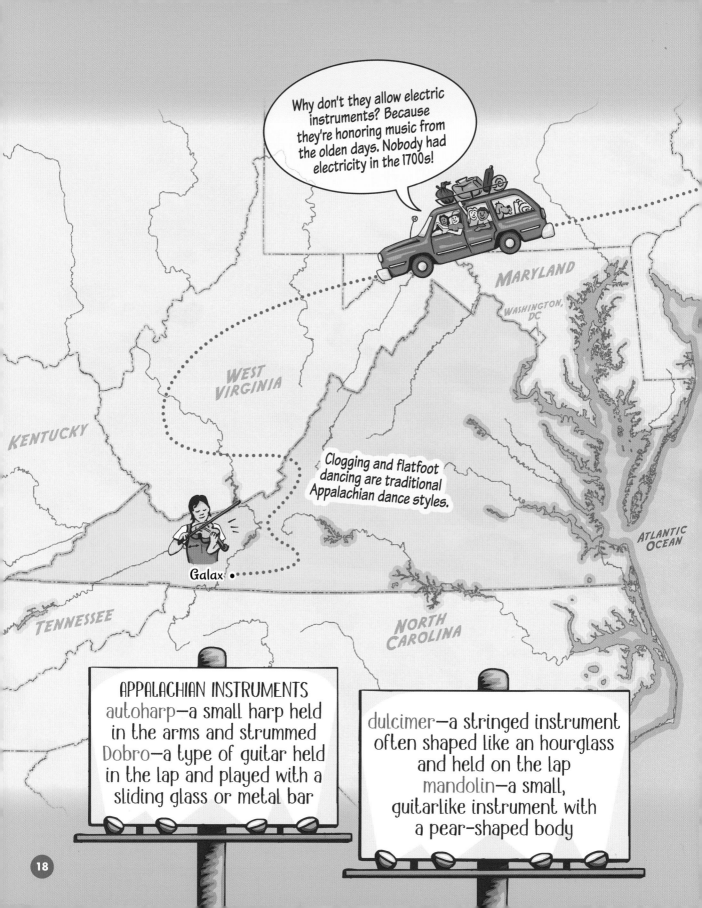

THE OLD FIDDLERS' CONVENTION IN GALAX

Check out the Old Fiddlers' Convention in Galax. You'll see and hear a lot more than fiddling! There are folk singers and flatfoot dancers. Some people play fiddles, banjos, and guitars. Others play instruments you may never have seen before. These include autoharps, mandolins, Dobros, and dulcimers.

Folk music and dancing are old Virginia **traditions**. They are folk arts of the Appalachian Region. Settlers came there from England, Scotland, and Ireland. They brought their music and dances with them. Over time, these arts took on new qualities. People added African American and Native American musical elements, such as rhythms and musical patterns. Today, music lovers are keeping these traditions alive.

Galax is home to the Blue Ridge Music Center.

Fiddles are used in many kinds of music, including bluegrass.

YORKTOWN AND THE REVOLUTIONARY WAR

How did colonial soldiers live? How did their guns work? How did they get the food they needed? Just stop by the American Revolution Museum at Yorktown. Guides show you all about soldiers' lives.

Yorktown was an important place in colonial history. The colonists wanted freedom from Great Britain. They fought the Revolutionary War (1775–1783). General George Washington led the Continental Army.

Many battles were fought in Virginia. The final battle took place at Yorktown. Britain's Lord Cornwallis surrendered there in 1781. Then the colonies became the United States of America. General Washington became the first president.

Watch reenactments of the Siege of Yorktown at Yorktown Battlefield.

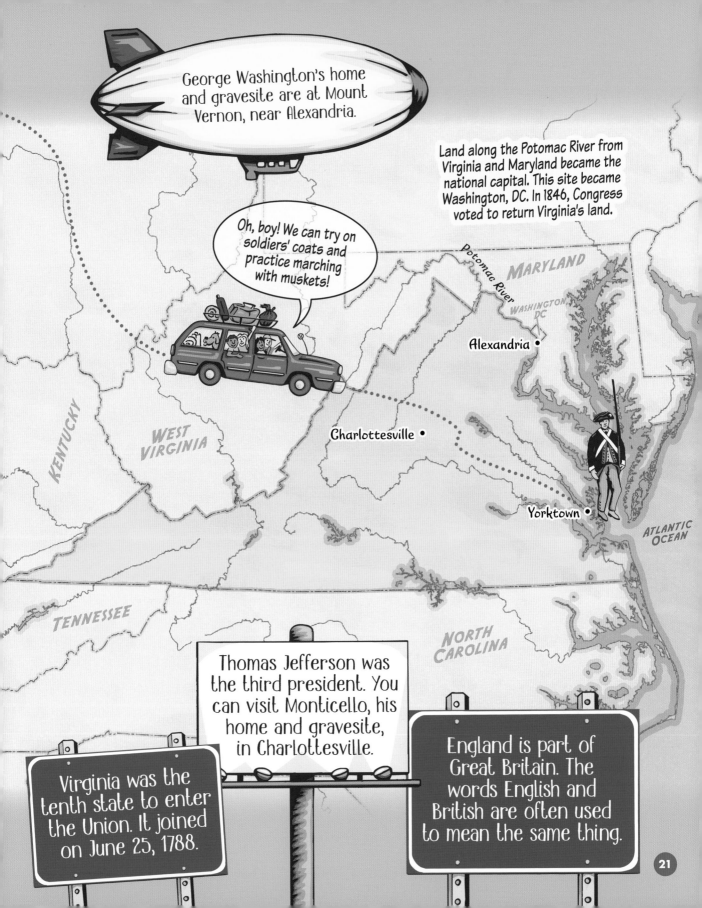

George Washington's home and gravesite are at Mount Vernon, near Alexandria.

Land along the Potomac River from Virginia and Maryland became the national capital. This site became Washington, DC. In 1846, Congress voted to return Virginia's land.

Oh, boy! We can try on soldiers' coats and practice marching with muskets!

Thomas Jefferson was the third president. You can visit Monticello, his home and gravesite, in Charlottesville.

Virginia was the tenth state to enter the Union. It joined on June 25, 1788.

England is part of Great Britain. The words English and British are often used to mean the same thing.

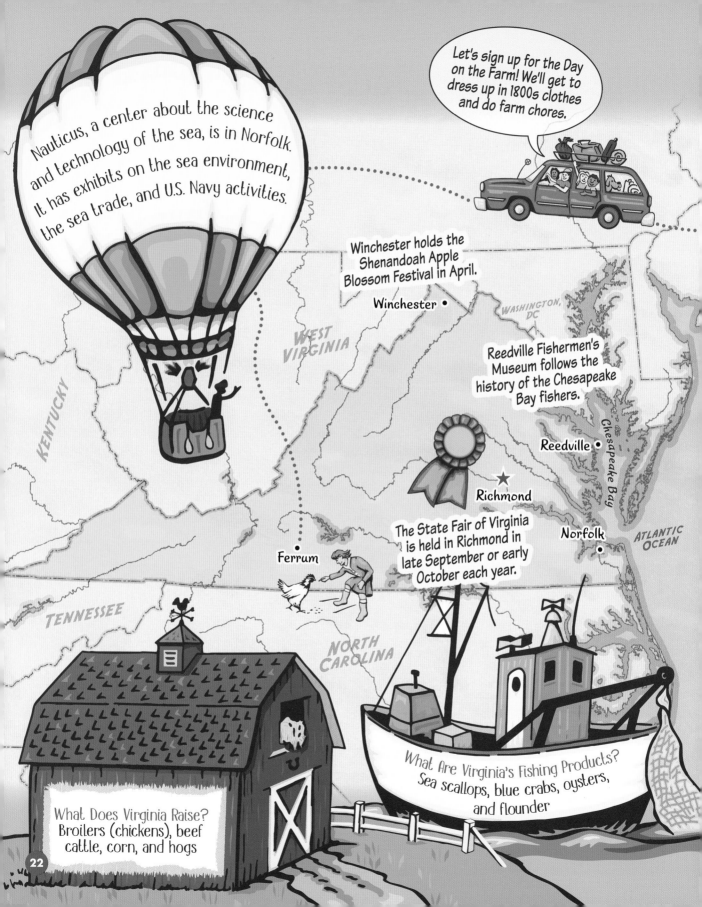

Blue Ridge Farm Museum in Ferrum is a great place to visit. It's just like a farm in 1800. Costumed workers are doing their daily chores. They're cooking meals or tending the farm animals. You can even help with some of these activities.

Many Virginians used to farm. Farming is still the state's largest industry. Today, many farmers raise chickens and beef cattle. These animals are the leading farm products. Growing tobacco was once Virginia's major industry. Tobacco is still the top crop today.

Fishing is a big industry in Virginia. Fishers haul in tons of oysters and crabs. They catch lots of fish, too!

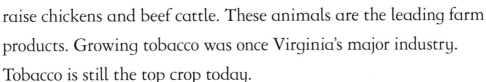

Blue Ridge Farm Museum has historic log barns and cabins.

APPOMATTOX COURT HOUSE AND THE CIVIL WAR

Get enlisted to fight in the Civil War. Learn how to set up camp. Go through military **drills** with a soldier. Use the skills you've learned in a mock battle. You're taking part in the Appomattox Court House Summer Day Camp!

This event takes place at Appomattox Court House. The courthouse is now part of a historical park. It's an important Civil War (1861–1865) site. The states fought this war over slavery.

Northern states formed the Union side. They wanted to outlaw slavery. Southern states made up the **Confederacy**. Confederate states wanted to keep slavery. Virginia joined the Confederate side. In the end, the Union forces won. The surrender was signed at Appomattox Court House.

Learn more in the visitor center in the Appomattox Court House.

Virginia was the site of 123 Civil War battles.

Let's check out the McLean House! That's where the surrender was signed.

Manassas National Battlefield Park is near Manassas. Two important Civil War battles were fought there. They're called the Battles of Manassas, or the Battles of Bull Run.

MARYLAND

WASHINGTON, DC

WEST VIRGINIA

Manassas •

The White House and Museum of the Confederacy is in Richmond. It has many exhibits on the South and the Confederacy.

KENTUCKY

Appomattox •

★ Richmond

Richmond was the capital of the Confederacy from May 1861 to April 1865.

ATLANTIC OCEAN

TENNESSEE

NORTH CAROLINA

Counties in western Virginia stayed in the Union. They formed the state of West Virginia in 1863.

Confederate generals Robert E. Lee, Stonewall Jackson, and James Ewell Brown "Jeb" Stuart were Virginians.

Confederate general Robert E. Lee surrendered to Union general Ulysses S. Grant on April 9, 1865.

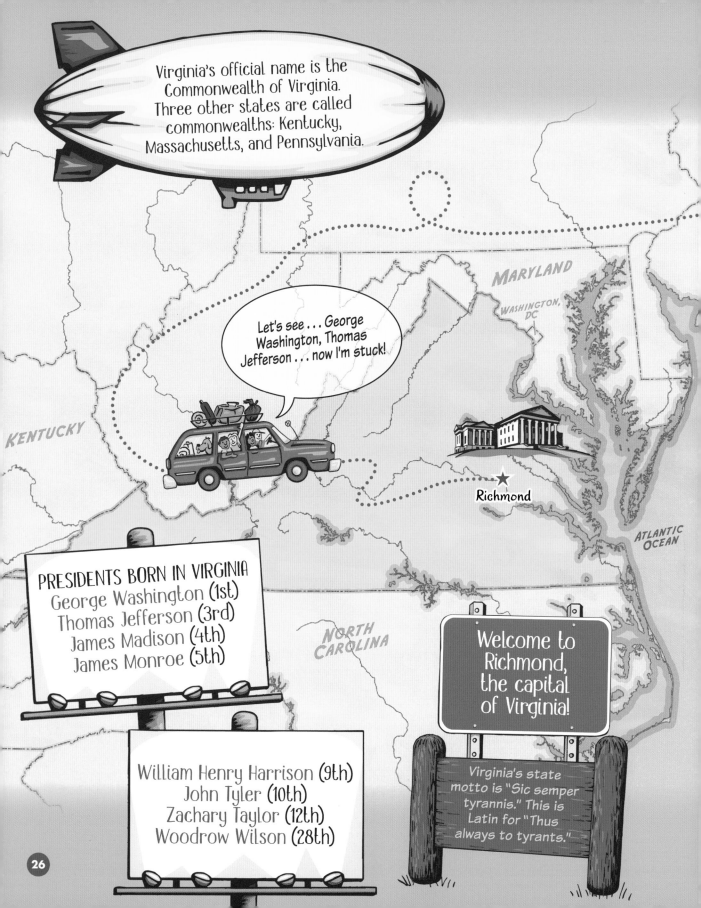

THE STATE CAPITOL IN RICHMOND

Do you know what all the presidents looked like? You can test yourself on eight of them. Their statues are in the state capitol. Why are they there? All eight were born in Virginia!

The capitol is the center of state government. Inside are many state government offices. Virginia's government has three branches. One branch makes the state's laws. It's called the General Assembly. Another branch carries out the laws. The governor heads this branch. The third branch is made up of judges. They decide whether laws have been broken.

Thomas Jefferson helped design Virginia's capitol.

INVENTORS HALL OF FAME IN ALEXANDRIA

Think about bicycles, toys, and cameras. Someone invented each one. Inventors must get a **patent** or **trademark**. These help prevent illegal copying.

Want to learn all about inventions? Just visit the National Inventors Hall of Fame and Museum in Alexandria.

Inventions helped Virginia's **industries** grow. In the 1880s, Virginia was making many products. These included cigarettes, cotton cloth, and ships.

By the mid-1900s, Washington, DC, was filling up. As a result many U.S. government offices were opened in Virginia. One is the U.S. Patent and Trademark Office, which houses the Hall of Fame.

Learn about incredible inventors at the National Inventors Hall of Fame and Museum.

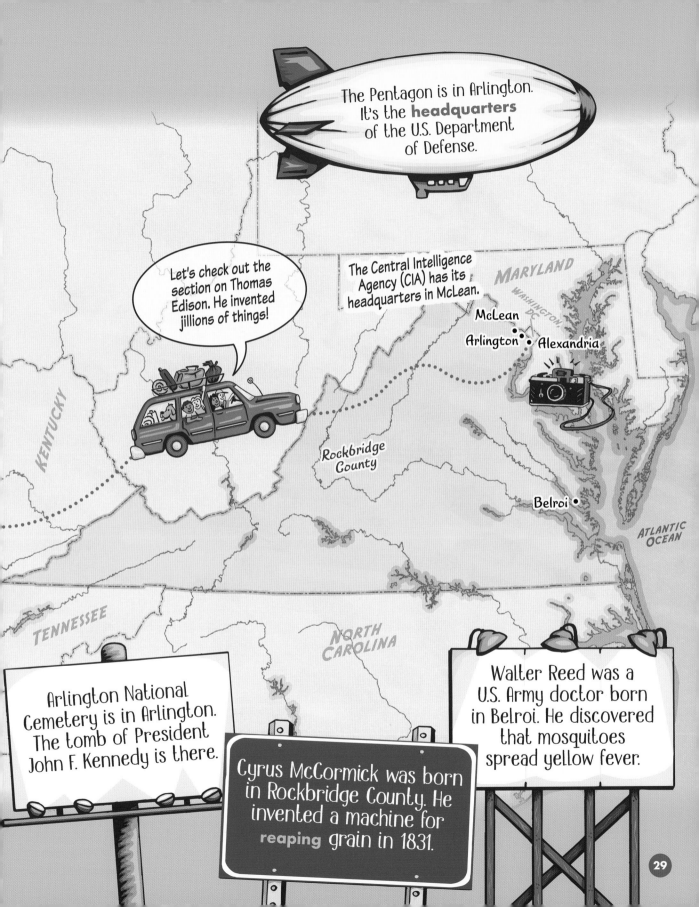

In 2016, 8,411,808 people lived in Virginia. It's the 12th-largest state by population.

These people are taking the **oath** of citizenship. They swear to support the United States and its laws.

MARYLAND

WASHINGTON, DC

WEST VIRGINIA

KENTUCKY

The Frontier Culture Museum is in Staunton. Its farms reflect the cultures of early Virginia immigrants.

Staunton •

• Charlottesville

Virginia Beach

ATLANTIC OCEAN

Norfolk •

Chesapeake •

Filipinos are people from the Philippine Islands in the Pacific Ocean.

NORTH CAROLINA

POPULATION OF LARGEST CITIES
Virginia Beach.............452,745
Norfolk.....................246,393
Chesapeake.................235,429

The process by which a foreign citizen becomes a U.S. citizen is called naturalization.

Monticello is near Charlottesville.

BECOMING CITIZENS AT MONTICELLO

The place is Monticello, Thomas Jefferson's home. The day is the Fourth of July. People from Latin America, Europe, Asia, and Africa are here. Today, they become citizens of the United States. This ceremony takes place every year. It's a big moment for those who attend.

Virginia has always been a place for **immigrants**. Early settlers came from England, Ireland, and Germany. Later, people came from all over the world. Today, Virginians have roots in many lands. Thousands of Filipinos live around Norfolk. People of many **cultures** live in northern Virginia. They include Vietnamese, **Hispanic**, and Korean people.

People from around the world become American citizens at Monticello.

MAKING POTATO CHIPS IN MOUNT JACKSON

Large windows give you the inside scoop on potato-chip making. Watch the chips fry and see workers stir the chips with long poles. You're visiting Route 11 Potato Chips in Mount Jackson! Virginia has lots of other factories, too.

Tobacco products are the leading factory goods. Soft drinks are major products, as well. Many Virginia factories make medicines. Others make plastics or cars.

Virginia also makes boats and big ships. Newport News, Norfolk, and Portsmouth are shipbuilding cities.

Sample fresh chips at Route 11 Potato Chips.

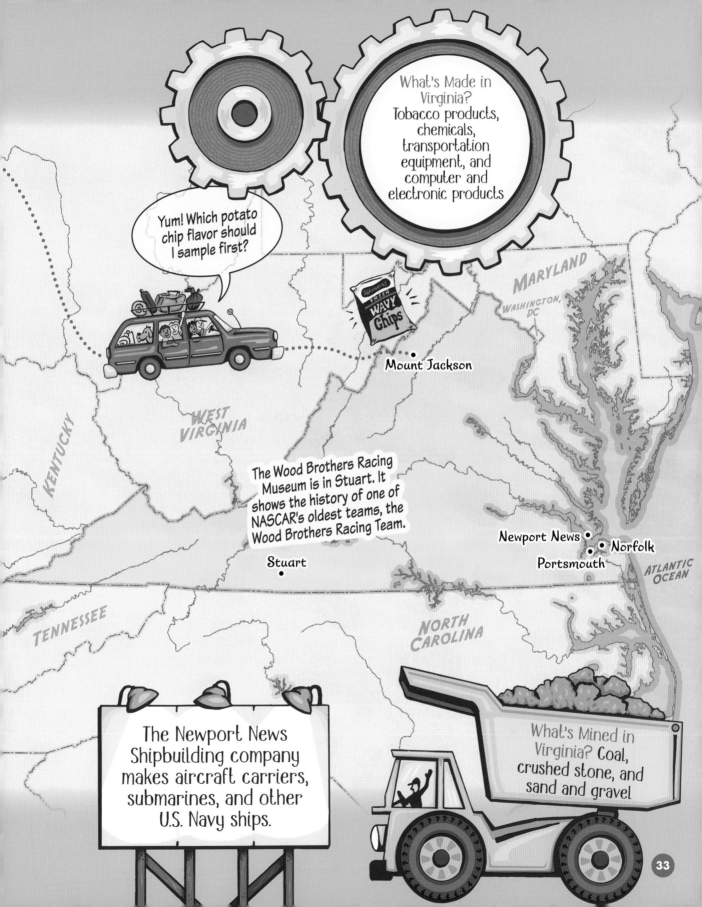

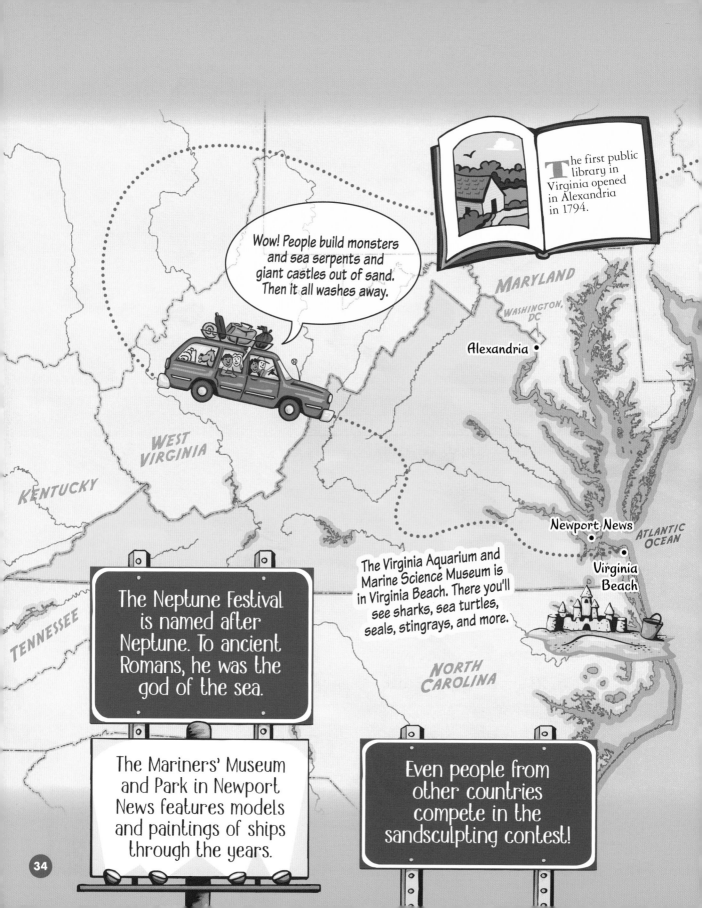

The first public library in Virginia opened in Alexandria in 1794.

Wow! People build monsters and sea serpents and giant castles out of sand. Then it all washes away.

MARYLAND

WASHINGTON, DC

Alexandria •

WEST VIRGINIA

KENTUCKY

Newport News •

ATLANTIC OCEAN

Virginia Beach •

The Virginia Aquarium and Marine Science Museum is in Virginia Beach. There you'll see sharks, sea turtles, seals, stingrays, and more.

The Neptune Festival is named after Neptune. To ancient Romans, he was the god of the sea.

TENNESSEE

NORTH CAROLINA

The Mariners' Museum and Park in Newport News features models and paintings of ships through the years.

Even people from other countries compete in the sandsculpting contest!

BUILDING SAND CASTLES IN VIRGINIA BEACH

Are you good at building sand castles? Then enter the International Sandsculpting Championship! It's part of Virginia Beach's Neptune Festival. People come with buckets and shovels. Some bring wheelbarrows, ladders, and garden tools! They build amazing things out of sand.

Virginia Beach is a popular vacation spot. People enjoy many activities along the coast. They go swimming, boating, or fishing. They even take whale-watching tours.

Some people head for Virginia's rugged mountains. They hike, watch wildlife, or explore caves. Others visit museums and historic sites. Whatever you enjoy, you'll find it in Virginia!

A large statue of Neptune greets visitors at Virginia Beach.

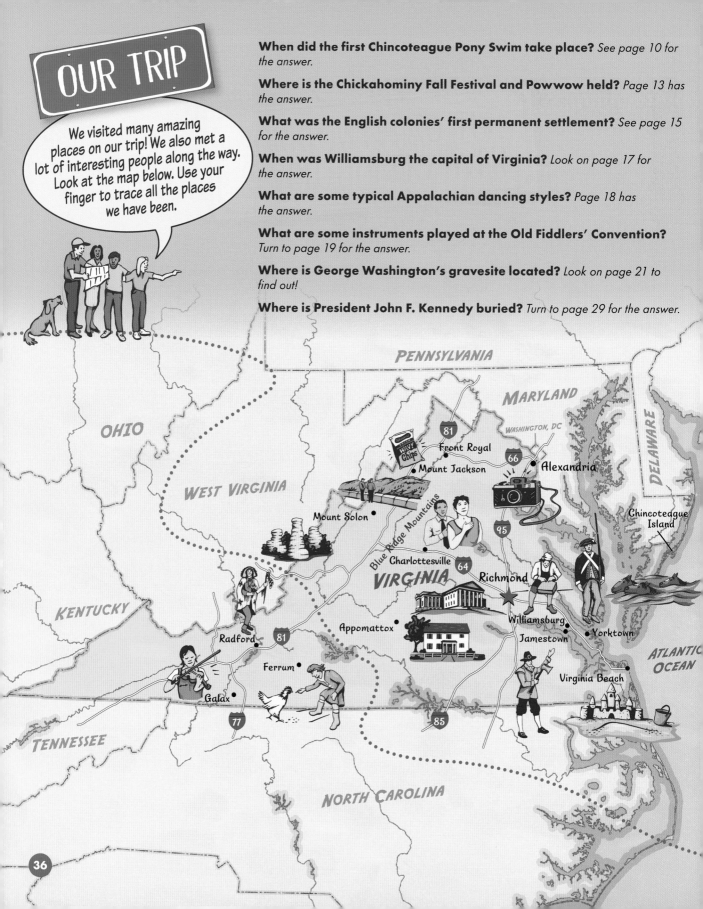

OUR TRIP

We visited many amazing places on our trip! We also met a lot of interesting people along the way. Look at the map below. Use your finger to trace all the places we have been.

When did the first Chincoteague Pony Swim take place? *See page 10 for the answer.*

Where is the Chickahominy Fall Festival and Powwow held? *Page 13 has the answer.*

What was the English colonies' first permanent settlement? *See page 15 for the answer.*

When was Williamsburg the capital of Virginia? *Look on page 17 for the answer.*

What are some typical Appalachian dancing styles? *Page 18 has the answer.*

What are some instruments played at the Old Fiddlers' Convention? *Turn to page 19 for the answer.*

Where is George Washington's gravesite located? *Look on page 21 to find out!*

Where is President John F. Kennedy buried? *Turn to page 29 for the answer.*

OHIO

PENNSYLVANIA

MARYLAND

DELAWARE

WEST VIRGINIA

WASHINGTON, DC

Front Royal

Mount Jackson

Alexandria

Mount Solon

Blue Ridge Mountains

Charlottesville

Chincoteague Island

VIRGINIA

Richmond

KENTUCKY

Radford

Appomattox

Williamsburg

Yorktown

ATLANTIC OCEAN

Ferrum

Jamestown

Galax

Virginia Beach

TENNESSEE

NORTH CAROLINA

State flag

State seal

STATE SYMBOLS

State beverage: Milk

State bird: Cardinal

State boat: Chesapeake Bay deadrise

State dog: American foxhound

State fish: Brook trout

State flower: Dogwood blossom

State folk dance: Square dance

State fossil: *Chesapecten jeffersonius*

State insect: Tiger swallowtail butterfly

State popular song: "Sweet Virginia Breeze"
by Robin Thompson and Steve Bassett

State shell: Oyster shell

State tree: Flowering dogwood

STATE SONG

"OUR GREAT VIRGINIA"
words by Mike Greenly, music by Jim Papoulis

You'll always be our great Virginia.
You're the birthplace of the nation:
Where history was changed forever.
Today, your glory stays, as we build
   tomorrow.

I fill with pride at all you give us—
Rolling hills, majestic mountains,
From the Shenandoah to the Atlantic,
Rivers wide and forests tall, all in one
   Virginia.

For each of us here in Virginia,
From farm to city dweller,
All of us, we stand together.
We're yours, we all are yours—
Across our great Virginia.
You'll always be our great Virginia.

That was a great trip! We have traveled all over Virginia! There are a few places that we didn't have time for, though. Next time, we plan to visit Thomas Jefferson's Poplar Forest near Bedford. This was his retreat home. Archaeologists and architects are working to fully restore the house and land.

FAMOUS PEOPLE

Ashe, Arthur (1943-1993), tennis champion

Bullock, Sandra (1964-), actor

Clark, William (1770-1838), explorer

Douglas, Gabby (1995-), Olympic gymnast

Fitzgerald, Ella (1917-1996), jazz singer

Henry, Patrick (1736-1799), patriot during the American Revolution

Iverson, Allen (1975-), basketball player

Jefferson, Thomas (1743-1826), 3rd U.S. president

Lee, Robert E. (1807-1870), commander of the Confederate army

Lewis, Meriwether (1774-1809), explorer

Madison, James (1751-1836), 4th U.S. president

Mourning, Alonzo (1970-), basketball player

Pocahontas (ca. 1595-1617), Powhatan who helped the English settlers

Scott, Winfield (1786-1866), hero of the Mexican War

Smith, Bruce (1963-), football player

Turner, Nat (1800-1831), preacher and slave

Washington, Booker T. (1856-1915), educator and founder of Tuskegee Institute

Washington, George (1732-1799), first U.S. president

Williams, Pharrell (1973-), singer, songwriter, and producer

Wilson, Russell (1988-), football player

Wilson, Woodrow (1856-1924), 28th U.S. president

Wright, David (1982-), baseball player

WORDS TO KNOW

apothecary (uh-PO-thuh-kair-ee) an early type of drugstore; also, the druggist working there

colonists (KOL-uh-nists) people who settle a new land for their home country

colony (KOL-uh-nee) a land settled and governed by another country

confederacy (kuhn-FED-ur-uh-see) a group of states with a shared goal

cultures (KUHL-churz) the customs, beliefs, and ways of life of various groups of people

drills (DRILZ) military exercises

headquarters (HED-kwor-turz) the home office of an organization

Hispanic (hiss-PAN-ik) having roots in Spanish-speaking lands

immigrants (IM-uh-gruhnts) people who move into another country

industries (IN-duh-streez) types of business

oath (OHTH) a solemn promise

patent (PAT-uhnt) the legal right to make and sell an invention

peninsula (puh-NIN-suh-luh) a piece of land almost completely surrounded by water

reaping (REEP-ing) cutting grain at harvest

trademark (TRADE-mark) words or symbols indicating the company that legally owns a product

traditions (truh-DISH-uhnz) customs passed down for many years

TO LEARN MORE

IN THE LIBRARY

Bailer, Darice. *George Washington*. Mankato, MN: The Child's World, 2017.

Cunningham, Kevin. *The Virginia Colony*. New York, NY: Children's Press, 2012.

Parker, Janice. *Virginia: The Old Dominion*. New York, NY: AV2, 2012.

ON THE WEB

Visit our Web site for links about Virginia:

childsworld.com/links

Note to Parents, Teachers, and Librarians: We routinely verify our Web links to make sure they are safe and active sites. So encourage your readers to check them out!

PLACES TO VISIT OR CONTACT

Virginia Historical Society

vahistorical.org

428 North Boulevard

Richmond, VA 23220

804/358-4901

For more information about the history of Virginia

Virginia Is for Lovers

virginia.org

901 East Cary Street, Suite 900

Richmond, VA 23219

804/545-5500

For more information about traveling in Virginia

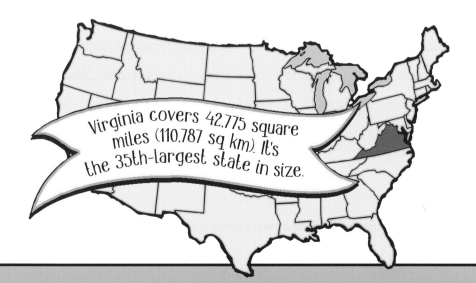

Virginia covers 42,775 square miles (110,787 sq km). It's the 35th-largest state in size.

INDEX

Bye, Old Dominion State.
We had a great time.
We'll come back soon!